Page 10

Page 14

Page 16

Page 17

9 10 11 1 12 7 6 4 13 2 3 5 8

Page 21

Page 23

Page 24

Page 29

Page 27

2

3

1

Page 30

Page 44

Page 47

Page 34

Page 45

Page 49

Page 54

Page 55

Page 56

Page 57

Page 61

Page 62

My First Big Sticker Book

BuzzPop

Stars in Space
Help the spaceship travel to its home planet. How many stars does it pass along the way?

START

FINISH

ANSWER: ____

Answer on Page 63

Pond Pals
Find the stickers to complete this scene.

3

Ship, Ahoy!

Find two more pirate ships on your sticker sheets. Add them to the scene, so the pirates can trade treasure.

Time for T. rex
Can you make this giant
dinosaur colorful?

Answer on Page 63

Unicorn

Fairy

Mermaid

Pegasus

Magical Matching
Draw a line to match each
magical creature to its name.

Answers on Page 63

Move Your Body

These friends like to exercise together. Find the correct sticker to complete each pattern.

Answers on Page 63

Starry Night
What a beautiful night sky! How many stars do you see?

Your answer: _____

Answer on Page 63

9

Busy Yard

Use your stickers to add a bird, a bug, a snail, a skunk, and a worm to this scene.

Woof!
Draw a silly face on the balloon puppy.
Then color it to make it your own.

Where's the Wool?
Help the kitten find the right path to its yarn.

Answer on Page 63

Buzzz!
These busy bees are working on their hive. How many can you count?

Your answer: _____

Cock-a-doodle-doo!
Color the picture. Then use your stickers to add one hen and two baby chicks to the farm.

So Many Monkeys
Circle the one that's upside down, and color the rest that are hanging around.

Answer on Page 63

Bird  **Black**

Bear **Green**

Frog  **Yellow**

Cat **Blue**

Snake  **Brown**

Colorful Critters
Place the correct animal sticker on the circle next to its name. Then draw a line from each animal sticker to its color.

Answers on Page 63

Autumn!
It's time for leaves to fall off trees.
Can you count them?

How many are on the branches? _____

How many are falling down? _____

How many are on the ground? _____

Answers on Page 63

Stripes and Spots
Oh, no! The zebra and giraffe have lost their patterns! Can you color them in?

Under the Sea
Trace this fish along the
dashed outlines. Then
color it any way you wish!

Barnyard Buddies

It's a busy day on the farm. Find the animal stickers to complete this scene.

Happy Birthday!
Today is a special day. Use the dots as a color guide to create a yummy cake.

On a Mission!
Use your stickers to give the astronaut
some planets to discover.

Yo-ho-ho!
Find three jewels and one crown on your sticker sheets, and put them in the treasure chest.

24

I Spy a Candy Shop
This store is filled with yummy treats.
Make four gumballs green, two lollipops
yellow, and one cupcake pink. Then color
the rest however you want.

Hungry for Books!
Help this worm eat its way through the apple to find some more books.

Start

Finish

Answer on Page 63

Monkey See, Monkey Eat!
Find the numbered stickers for this page. Then match them to the picture to give the monkey a treat.

Fall Season
Circle the scene that is a little different.

Answer on Page 64

Sundae, Fun Day
Find the banana split sticker and place it on the circle. Then color the sundae to match the sticker.

Deep in the Ocean

These sea creatures are waiting for their buddies.
Add stickers for a whale, a seahorse, and a jellyfish,
so they can go for a swim together.

Silly Monster!
Can you make this monster's
fur look funny and special?

Snow Puppy
This little doggie loves to play in the snow.
How many snowballs does he have?

The dog has _____ snowballs.

Answer on Page 64

Who says "Quack"?
Connect the dots to find out.

You Can Do It!
Help the cow jump over the moon. Use your stickers to complete the puzzle.

Great Job!
You just won a trophy! Write your name on it.

Hooray for Hippos!
Circle the hippo that is a little different.
Then color them all.

Answer on Page 64

Nice Kitty!
Connect the dots to see who will grow up to be King of the Jungle!

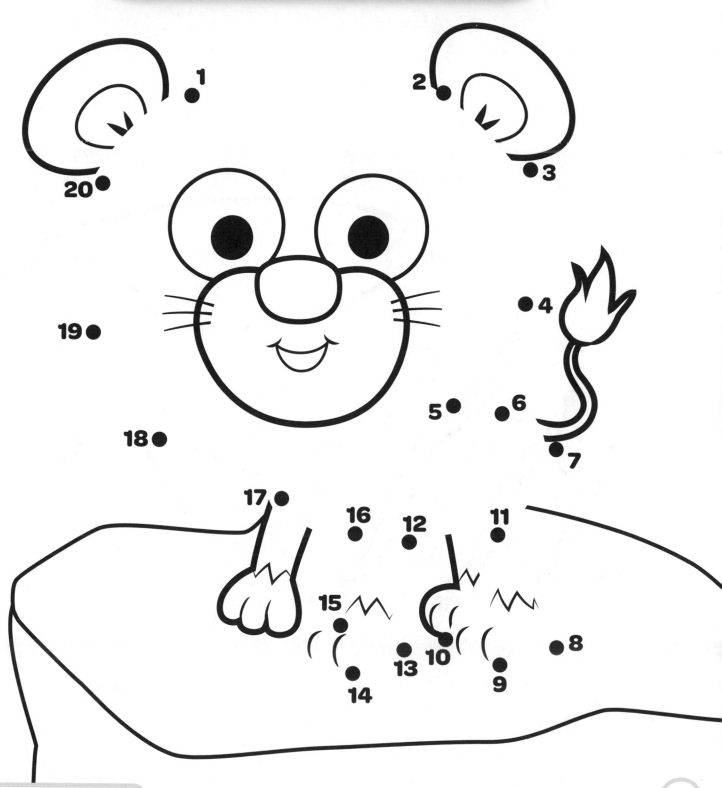

Answer on Page 64

See the Seashell
Connect the dots to find something pretty from the ocean.

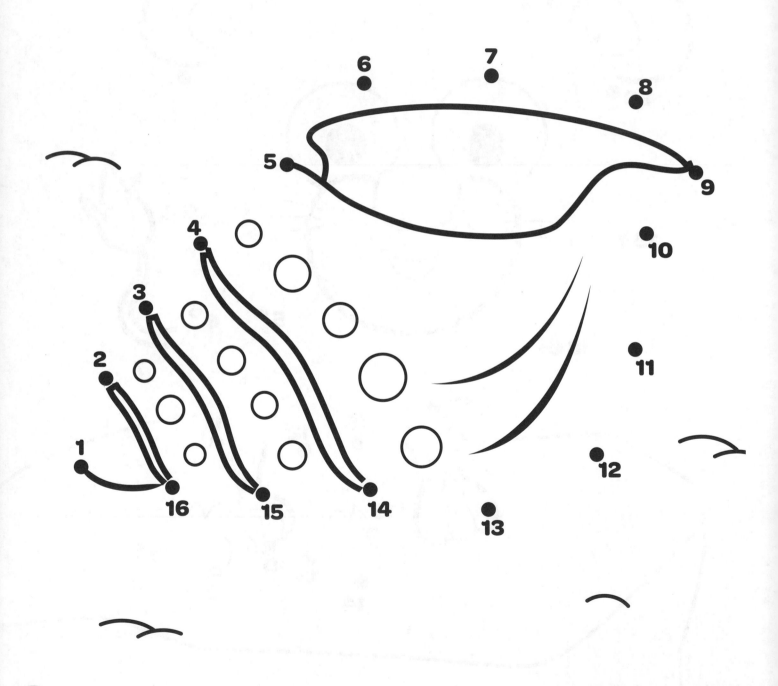

Answer on Page 64

More Bubbles, Please!
This puppy likes his bath extra bubbly.
Color the picture and draw as many
bubbles as you can on the page.

Flutter, Flutter!
Make each butterfly a different color.

Unicorn Rainbow
Use the dots as a color guide to make this unicorn's rainbow bright!

Pretty Flowers
Can you color the last tulip in each row to complete the pattern?

Answer on Page 64

Friendly Elephant
Trace around the lines of this elephant to complete the picture. Then color it any way you like.

43

Hungry Rabbit
Find more carrots for the bunny to eat on your sticker sheets.

Smile!
This friendly fairy can make flowers smile. Use your stickers to put a smiling face on both flowers.

Down in the Deep
Circle the submarine that is a little different.
Then color them all.

Answer on Page 64

From Caterpillar to Butterfly
This caterpillar will turn into a butterfly one day.
Find four butterfly stickers and place them on the page.

Dragon Shadows
Can you match the dragons to their shadows?
Write the correct letter on each line.

Answers on Page 64

Giant Chef

This giant wants to make a fresh apple pie. Use your stickers to add some apples to the tree for him to pick.

Out of This World!
It's almost time to blast off. Finish the drawing so the rocket can soar!

Answer on Page 64

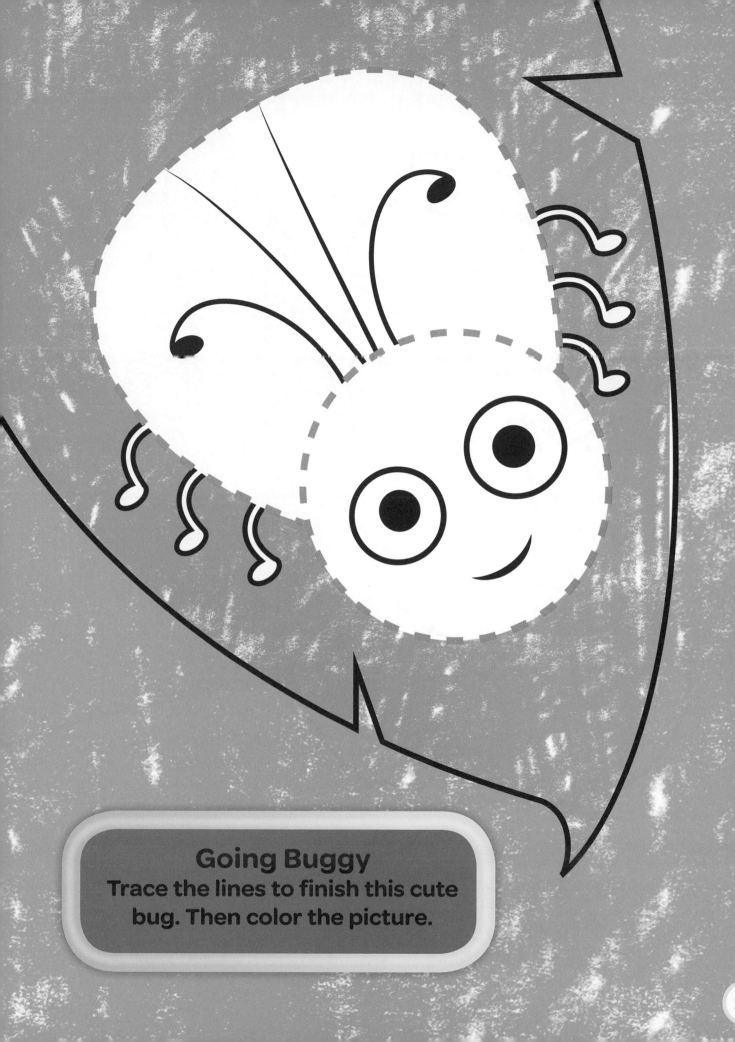

Going Buggy
Trace the lines to finish this cute
bug. Then color the picture.

51

Snow Business
This snowman isn't finished.
Use crayons to give him some color!

A Smiling Shark

How many teeth does this smiling shark have?
Color each tooth a different color as you count.

Answer on Page 64

Your answer:

53

Line of Robots
Which robot is the smallest? Which is the biggest?
Find your robot stickers and put them in size order.

54

Just Add Sprinkles
This yummy cupcake is almost ready to eat.
Add sprinkle stickers to make it special!

Knight in Shining Armor

The knight can't go to battle dressed like this.
Use your stickers to give him his helmet, armor,
shield, and sword.

Fly High in the Sky
Color this helicopter red.
Find stickers of more things
that fly to add to the page.

Spinning Spider

What kind of web should the spider make? Draw it here.

Go, Go, Go!
Which picture doesn't go with the others? Cross it out.

Answer on Page 64

Lots of Gumballs
Oh, what a lovely gumball machine!
Make one gumball orange, three gumballs blue,
four gumballs yellow, and five gumballs green.

Surf's Up!
Use your stickers to decorate the
girl's surfboard so she can catch
waves in style.

In the Yard
The puppy is looking for his friends.
Use your stickers to add a rabbit, a snail,
and a bird, so they can play.